A Note to Parents and Teachers

DK READERS is a compelling reading programme for children. The programme is designed in conjunction with leading literacy experts, including Cliff Moon M.Ed., who has spent many years as a teacher and teacher educator specializing in reading. Cliff Moon has written more than 160 books for children and teachers. He is series editor to Collins Big Cat.

Beautiful illustrations and superb full-colour photographs combine with engaging, easy-to-read stories to offer a fresh approach to each subject in the series. Each DK READER is guaranteed to capture a child's interest while developing his or her reading skills, general knowledge, and love of reading.

The five levels of DK READERS are aimed at different reading abilities, enabling you to choose the books that are exactly right for your child:

Pre-level 1: Learning to read
Level 1: Beginning to read
Level 2: Beginning to read alone
Level 3: Reading alone
Level 4: Proficient readers

The "normal" age at which a child begins to read can be anywhere from three to eight years old. Adult participation through the lower levels is very helpful for providing encouragement, discussing storylines and sounding out unfamiliar words.

No matter which level you select, you can be sure that you are helping your child learn to read, then read to learn!

DK

LONDON, NEW YORK, MUNICH,
MELBOURNE, AND DELHI

DK LONDON

Series Editor Deborah Lock
Art Director Martin Wilson
Production Editor Francesca Wardell
Jacket Designer Martin Wilson

Reading Consultant
Cliff Moon, M.Ed.

DK DELHI

Senior Editor Priyanka Nath
Senior Art Editor Rajnish Kashyap
Assistant Editor Deeksha Saikia
Assistant Designer Dhirendra Singh
DTP Designer Anita Yadav
Picture Researcher Sumedha Chopra
Managing Editor Alka Thakur Hazarika
Managing Art Editor Romi Chakraborty

First published in Great Britain by
Dorling Kindersley Limited
80 Strand, London, WC2R 0RL

Copyright © 2013 Dorling Kindersley Limited
A Penguin Company

10 9 8 7 6 5 4 3 2 1
001—187465—June/2013

A CIP catalogue record for this book
is available from the British Library
ISBN: 978-1-40932-660-1

Colour reproduction by Colourscan, Singapore
Printed and bound in China by L Rex Printing Co., Ltd.

The publisher would like to thank the following for their kind permission to
reproduce their photographs:

(Key: a-above; b-below/bottom; c-centre; f-far; l-left; r-right; t-top)

2 **Corbis:** Imaginechina (br); Ken Paul / All Canada Photos (tr). **Great Southern
Railway:** (clb). David Gubler (cla). 3 **Dreamstime.com:** Tommaso79 (cb). 4-5
SuperStock: age fotostock (b). 6 **Corbis:** Christophe Boisvieux. 7 **Dorling
Kindersley:** Rough Guides (tr). **SuperStock:** Xavier Forés / age fotostock (b). 8
Alamy Images: Matthew Clarke (clb). 8-9 **Orient-Express Hotels Trains &
Cruises:** (b). 9 **Orient-Express Hotels Trains & Cruises:** (tr). 10-11 **Alamy
Images:** Keren Su / China Span (b). 12-13 **SuperStock:** Wolfgang Kaehler (b).
13 **Alamy Images:** Andrew Gransden (cla). **Corbis:** Richard Ross (br). 14-15
Great Southern Railway: (t). 16 **Alamy Images:** JTB Media Creation, Inc. (bl).
17 **Alamy Images:** Image Gap. 18-19 **Getty Images:** Iris Kuerschner / Look (b).
19 **Alamy Images:** Sonderegger Christof / Prisma Bildagentur AG (t).
Dreamstime.com: Nui7711 (br). 20-21 David Gubler (t). 21 seat61.com. 22
Corbis: Ken Paul / All Canada Photos. **Photoshot:** Mel Longhurst (bl). 23 **Alamy
Images:** Jack Sullivan (t). 24-25 **Getty Images:** Gavin Hellier / The Image Bank
(b). 25 **Corbis:** Michael S. Yamashita (t). 26-27 **Getty Images:** Denis Charlet /
AFP (b). 28-29 **Dreamstime.com:** Mamahoohooba (b). 29 **Corbis:** Imaginechina
(t). 32 **Alamy Images:** Matthew Clarke (tl). **Corbis:** Richard Ross (cl). **Dorling
Kindersley:** Rough Guides (clb). **Dreamstime.com:** Nui7711 (cla). **Photoshot:**
Mel Longhurst (bl). 33 **Getty Images:** Erich Hafele / age fotostock (br)

Jacket images: Front: Corbis: Dan Sherwood / Design Pics

All other images © Dorling Kindersley
For further information see: www.dkimages.com

Discover more at
www.dk.com

DK READERS

BEGINNING 1 TO READ

Train Travel

Written by Deborah Lock

DK

A Dorling Kindersley Book

AROUND THE WORLD TICKET

DK

ROUND TRIP

NO.:54321

Tickets please!
Climb aboard!
Watch your step!
We are going on a trip of
a lifetime to see the world by train.

It's a slow start as we wind
our way up a mountain.
We're on a small train in India
and the ride will take
eight hours.

Puff!

Puff!

We have picked
up speed.
We are on
a steam train.

viaduct

We travel from the mountains
to the sea in Scotland.
This viaduct has 21 arches
and it's been standing
for more than 100 years.

Dinner is served!
We are on the famous
Orient Express.
We are travelling from city
to city in Europe.
A diesel engine pulls
the shiny old carriages.

carriages

Whoosh!
We zigzag through
the Andes mountains in Peru.

This track is called
the "Railroad in the Clouds".
It's the second-highest railway
in the world.

Sit back and relax.
We have a long trip ahead on
the longest railway in the world.

ВЛ10-866

We are travelling all the way across Russia.

Goods trains pull more than 200,000 containers along this railway every year.

container

Look out for kangaroos!
We are travelling through
 the middle
of Australia.

We are on a very long train
called the Ghan.
It can pull lots of carriages.
It can be over a kilometre
(nearly a mile) long.

Are you tired?
This is the most comfortable
train in the world.
You have your own bedroom
on the Blue Train.
Come and sit in the lounge.
Enjoy the views
of South Africa.
Look! There's
a herd of elephants.

THE BLUE TRAIN
DIE BLOUTREIN
1955

Do you like bridges?
There are about 300 bridges on
this trip through the Swiss Alps.
The windows are huge so
you can see everything.
Click, clack!
The train uses cogwheels
to go up and down steep hills.

cogwheel

This is the Silver Lady.

It has a diesel engine.

It's like a silver thread streaking
through the USA.

At night, you can rest
in the sleeper carriages
or on a chair that leans back.

vistadome

Do you like long trips?
This train takes four days
to travel across Canada.
It goes across prairies, over rivers
and around lakes.
Sit on the top level.
You'll get the best views from
the vistadome.

Are you in a hurry?

This train in Japan is fast!

It's like a bullet, whizzing

from station to station.

This electric train gets its

power from the wire

above the track.

It's dark!

We are in a tunnel dug in
the rock under the sea.

The sea is between England
and France.
This fast train takes 35 minutes
to go through the long tunnel.

Our trip ends on the fastest
train yet!
Its rails are high above
the ground.
This train in China uses
magnet power.

What sort of trains will you travel on in the future?

Take a look at where
you have been.
Which was your favourite
train trip?

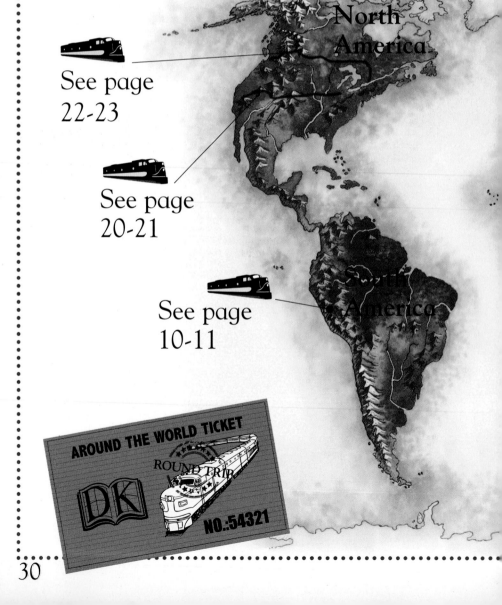

North
America

See page
22-23

See page
20-21

See page
10-11

South
America

AROUND THE WORLD TICKET
ROUND TRIP
DK
NO.:54321

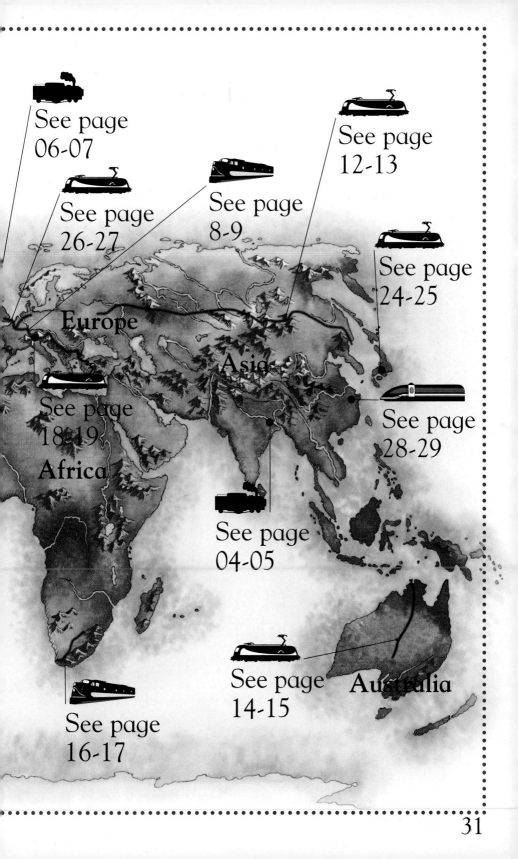

See page
06-07

See page
26-27

See page
8-9

See page
12-13

See page
24-25

Europe

Asia

See page
18-19

Africa

See page
28-29

See page
04-05

See page
14-15

Australia

See page
16-17

Glossary

Carriages
wheeled vehicles that carry many people

Cogwheel
a wheel with raised parts called teeth

Container
a large metal box that carries goods

Viaduct
a bridge with arches with a road or rails on top

Vistadome
a carriage with a glass dome on the top